how2become

Cabin Crew

Jessica Bond

Orders: Please contact How2become Ltd, Suite 2, 50 Churchill Square Business Centre, Kings Hill, Kent ME19 4YU.

Telephone: (44) 0845 643 1299 - Lines are open Monday to Friday 9am until 5pm. Fax: (44) 01732 525965. You can also order via the e-mail address info@how2become.co.uk

ISBN: 9781909229020

First published 2012

Typeset for How2become Ltd by Molly Hill, Canada.

Printed in Great Britain for How2become Ltd by Bell & Bain Ltd, 303 Burnfield Road, Thornliebank, Glasgow G46 7UQ.

CONTENTS

BE THE FIRST TO BE ALERTED WHEN CABIN CREW JOBS BECOME AVAILABLE!

Go to:

www.Cabin-Crew-Jobs.co.uk

to register your interest now…

Attend a Cabin Crew Training Course!

Go to:

www.cabincrewcourses.com

INTRODUCTION

Dear Sir/Madam,

Welcome to your new guide, how2become cabin crew. You will find this guide an invaluable resource in your pursuit to becoming cabin crew with any of the worldwide airlines. The information within this guide has been supplied by Jessica Bond, a serving senior cabin crew member with a major UK based airline. She has 14 years' experience in the role and is also a member of the cabin crew training and recruitment team within the airline industry.

The guide itself has been divided up in to useful sections to help you prepare effectively. To begin with, we will provide you with details about the role of cabin crew. This is extremely important, so please don't miss out this section. Once we have covered the role we will provide you with details about how to pass each element of the selection process and also the interview.

You won't achieve much in life without hard work, commitment

and dedication. Please take the time to prepare for the cabin crew selection process properly; it will be worth it!

If you need any further assistance with the selection process, please visit our award winning website:

www.how2become.com

Good luck and best wishes,

The How2become team

CHAPTER ONE
INTRODUCTION

A FEW THINGS YOU NEED TO KNOW

The career of a cabin crew member is considered by many to be a highly glamorous one and therefore it has a highly competitive selection process. Nevertheless, there is a down side which you are probably aware of but you need to know this before you apply.

You will, for the majority of time, be living out of a suitcase and working long hours. You will also find that you'll be away from loved ones for long periods of time, dependant on the airline you want to work for. Are you prepared to be away from friends, family and partner for weekend upon weekend? Are you prepared for working unsociable hours and eating when you are supposed to be sleeping, and sleeping when you should be eating?

These are all things that you need to consider and be aware of before applying. You'll no doubt be asked questions about the negative aspects of the job during the selection interview. Therefore, you need to be aware of what the negative aspects are, but more importantly, how to convince the panel that they are not a problem for you.

Within this guide we will show you exactly how to do this and how to answer all of your questions in a positive and confident manner.

CHOOSING THE CORRECT AIRLINE

Each airline is a different employer and therefore the quality of career you get from each of them will vary. It is the same when you fly with an airline either on business or when you are going on holiday. There are some you'd probably prefer not to fly with. This does not mean that they are a poor employer, but it is still very important that you choose your airline carefully.

There is a huge range of airlines to choose from and you must take your time when considering which one to apply for. Remember that you will probably be working for them for a long time, so you need to feel comfortable with your employer. Don't get carried away with just wanting to be a cabin crew member.

To begin with, you should ask yourself the following questions:

- Why do I want to be a cabin crew member?

- What do I expect to get out of my job?

- Do I mind being away from home for long periods of time?

- Is the image of the airline important to me?

- Is travelling important to me?

Once you have answered these questions honestly, you will begin to realise the type of airline you should approach.

WHY DO I WANT TO BECOME CABIN CREW?

The answer to this question is probably obvious. You want to travel the world, see different countries, meet new and exciting people and not have a boring 9 to 5 job like the majority of people? If these are your reasons for wanting to become a cabin crew member then you have chosen the right career.

However, when you are preparing for the selection process you need to change your attitude to what the career of a cabin crew member is all about. We will cover this in more detail later, but you need to realise that each airline is a business, solely interested in providing a high level of customer service to everyone who flies with them. If they provide an excellent level of service then people are more likely to fly with them again. This is where you come in! Have you ever flown with a particular airline and had a bad experience with the customer service? If you have, would you fly with them again? Hopefully you are beginning to understand where we are coming from here.

Start to think like the recruitment staff and focus on the type of people they are looking to recruit - those who are presentable, who are capable of providing a high level of service, are reliable and are customer focused.

WHAT DO I EXPECT TO GET OUT OF MY JOB?

This is another important question you should ask yourself. The answer you come up with will very much determine the type of airline you decide to apply for.

For instance, you may be looking to join an airline where you can travel and spend weeks away from home. If this is so, then you will be looking to apply to an airline where the long haul travel opportunities are more widely available.

However, if you are solely interested in the 'status' of a cabin crew career and do not want to travel for weeks at a time, you might want to consider a smaller, low budget airline where the travel distances are far less.

Only you and you alone will know what you want to get out of the job. It is important that you sit down and write out the things you hope to get out of the job on a piece of paper. Once you have done this, you can then start to take a look at the different types of airline that are most suited to your own personal needs.

DO I MIND BEING AWAY FROM HOME FOR LONG PERIODS OF TIME?

Another important question, but one you should take seriously. Many cabin crew members enjoy being away from home for weeks at a time and are constantly on the lookout for long haul flight opportunities. Take a look at your own personal circumstances. Do you have a partner? How would he/she feel about you being away from home for weeks at a time? How would you feel about being away from them?

If you are in the position that you have no ties or commitments, then your choice of work and airline will be an easy one. You

would find it easier to relocate closer to an airport, if required, without those ties that can hold you back.

How would you respond to an interview question of this nature? Could you provide examples of when you have been away from home for weeks at a time?

If you progress to the interview stage, you are more than likely to be asked a question of this nature.

You will need to demonstrate that you have thought long and hard about your choice of career and that you are prepared for the lengthy periods away from home.

IS THE IMAGE OF THE AIRLINE IMPORTANT TO ME?

Many people are not concerned about the image of the airline and are prepared to work for anybody, just to get the job. Ask yourself how important the image of the airline is to you and you will begin to understand the type of airline you want to apply for. There are many, low budget airlines who offer a fine level of service such as Ryan Air or Easy Jet.

However, you may wish to choose an airline with a different image such as British Airways or Virgin. Whichever one you decide to apply for, you will need to spend time studying all there is to know about that particular airline. You are almost guaranteed to be asked the question – 'Why do you want to join our airline?'

Within our 'useful contacts' section, we have provided a list of all the UK and International airlines' contact details, including their website addresses. When deciding which airline to apply for, spend a little time visiting their website and you will begin to get a feel as to what they are about.

Also, try asking friends and relatives what they think about the airline you are hoping to join. It is worth spending a little bit of time carrying out research on each airline, before committing to their selection process.

THE QUALITIES AND ATTRIBUTES OF CABIN CREW

These are extremely important to your role as a cabin crew member and the selection panel will be looking closely to see if you have them. Some of the qualities and attributes you will have naturally, but some of them will have to be acquired through practice and self-awareness.

Being DEPENDABLE is an important asset, especially when working as a team. Can the airline depend on you to turn up on time, or help out in any situation without being asked?

Do you take a PRIDE in your appearance and LOOK GOOD at all times, paying close attention to this important attribute?

What are your COMMUNICATION SKILLS like and are you an effective LISTENER?

Do you have a SENSE OF HUMOUR that is relevant and do you have a CARING ATTITUDE?

Are you MATURE and ORGANISED and can you demonstrate this to the selection panel?

On the following page we have provided you with a 'qualities and attributes' check list.

We advise that you look at each one carefully and write down, in the spaces provided, a situation where you have recently demonstrated each quality. Keep hold of the checklist as you will need this at a later point within the guide.

QUALITIES AND ATTRIBUTES CHECKLIST

[ ] dependable

[ ] understanding nature

[ ] caring

[ ] good sense of humour

[ ] taking pride in my appearance

[ ] motivated

[ ] enthusiastic

[ ] confident

[ ] a friendly nature

[ ] resilient

[ ] patient

[ ] mature outlook

[ ] organised

[ ] effective listener

[ ] good communicator

THE CABIN CREW SELECTION PROCESS

The cabin crew selection process is a difficult one to pass. Some candidates will find it harder than others, but the main thing to remember is that preparation and determination are key to your success.

Throughout the process you need to have a positive attitude and be confident in your own abilities. Of course, it is quite normal to feel apprehensive and nervous about the whole thing, but believing in yourself is essential.

The recruitment staff want to see a person who is confident (but not overconfident), reliable, committed and capable of dealing with difficult situations under pressure.

Therefore, the selection process has been designed to pick the best people for the job. The panel wants to choose the right people for their airline and their customers, which is why we have already told you to learn as much as possible about the one you want to join.

Most of the airlines have a 3 or 4 stage selection process which is detailed as follows.

STAGE ONE
The application form

STAGE 2
Documentation check and written tests

STAGE 3
Presentation and team assessments

STAGE 4
Formal interview

Each airline will vary slightly and it is important that you check the process first before planning your own preparation.

However, most of them are the same in the fact that you must pass each stage before progressing on to the next one. This means that it is vital you give 100% preparation and commitment to each stage. Each stage will normally last no longer than an hour and it is up to you to show the recruitment team, at every stage that you have the necessary qualities and attributes they are looking for. Apart from this, you will be required to demonstrate that you are capable of providing a level of customer service that is commensurate with their own standards, and show that you are dependable and will be able to work effectively in a team environment.

Obviously, this is quite a tall order for anyone regardless of their abilities, but if you plan each stage separately and break down each section into manageable portions, you will find it easier to handle.

Within this guide, we have broken down each of the selection areas separately for ease of use. We recommend you use one section at a time, as and when required.

Now let's take a look at the role of cabin crew and why an understanding of it is so important to helping you successfully pass the selection process.

CHAPTER TWO
THE ROLE OF CABIN CREW

Members of cabin crew have two main roles in their job; these are the safety of all the passengers and delivering great customer service. Cabin crew must have excellent interpersonal skills and these will be assessed throughout the selection process and will play an important part in your overall success.

The main focus of the role of cabin crew will always be on safety. A serious decision to evacuate the aircraft will always rest with the cockpit crew, but the cabin crew have the responsibility to oversee the evacuation and make sure that this is carried out according to the rules and procedures. The key role of cabin crew remains exactly as it always has been, and that is to keep all the passengers safe. The cabin crew are obliged to provide a safety briefing before the flight and to ensure that the passengers pay attention to it. If an

emergency situation arises the cabin crew are trained to help the passengers leave the aircraft swiftly and safely.

The cabin crew can make or break the reputation of an airline. They must be well-presented, be professional and make a good impression on passengers to encourage them to use the same airline again in the future. Airline companies know that passengers who experience bad customer service from cabin crew will change the airline they use; it's as simple as that.

This is why airline companies look for future cabin crew members who go to the assessment and interview with their eyes open to what the role of cabin crew is all about. They will want them to have shown an interest in the airline they have applied to, by knowing some history about the airline and where they fly to and from. They must be people who work well in a group and that have a friendly, confident and caring nature.

Before you attend the assessments and the interview it is vital that you understand the role and also understand the key qualities required to carry out the role competently. Let's take a look at a sample cabin crew job description and person specification.

SAMPLE CABIN CREW JOB DESCRIPTION

Cabin crew are required to provide exceptional customer service before, during and after the flight. In addition to this they are responsible for the safety of themselves, the safety of the other crew members and most importantly, the safety of the passengers. Cabin crew are trained to a very high standard to deal with emergency situations and to also administer first aid when necessary.

Cabin crew will carry out a number of pre-flight checks which include assessing all safety equipment and ensuring that the aisles and safety routes are clear from obstructions. They will then welcome on board the passengers and conduct a role call once all luggage is safely stored away and secured.

Following pre-flight safety briefings, cabin crew will serve refreshments to passengers, serve up drinks and also offer duty free goods and services. They will also deal with any passenger complaints and also deal with any other issues as and when they arise during the flight.

QUALITIES OF CABIN CREW

The different qualities required to become cabin crew are many and varied; however, the following will give you a very good idea of the type of qualities and attributes you will need in order to become successful in the role:

A safety-conscious attitude

You will be responsible for the safety of the passengers, and as such, you will need to work in an organised and safe manner. You will also need the ability to learn and retain large amounts of job-related information, procedures and training.

Flexibility

Cabin crew need to be very flexible in order to meet the demands and expectations of the role. Although you will receive your flying roster a few weeks before your scheduled flights, it is important that your diary is kept free to meet the roster. You may also be required to be on standby and be available to fly at short notice to cover sickness etc.

Calm approach and ability to work under pressure

Despite the perceived glamour of the role, cabin crew do work in sometimes extremely pressurised situations. Passengers can sometimes be very difficult to deal with and you will need a calm approach when dealing with passengers. You will need the ability to deal with complaints effectively whilst keeping your focus on the key elements of the role at all times.

Team working capabilities

Cabin crew very rarely work with the same people each day. You will find that you work with a large amount of different people during your career. Cabin crew teams vary one day to the next. Therefore, you must have the ability to work with everyone, regardless of their gender, background, age, sexual orientation or religious beliefs.

Pride in appearance

It goes without saying, but you must be capable of looking after yourself and taking a pride in your appearance. Some airlines will place more emphasis on this attribute than others.

Ability to follow procedures

Cabin crew must be able to work unsupervised and follow procedures religiously. Safety is absolutely paramount to the role and you will be expected to follow your training to the letter. You will have many rules and procedures to absorb during your training and therefore, an ability to learn and retain a large amount of job-related information is absolutely necessary.

Excellent customer service skills

Air cabin crew staff must have exceptional customer service skills. The competition within the airline industry is extremely fierce and as such, each airline is competing for every

passenger. One of the most important elements of customer satisfaction is the level of service a passenger receives from the airline cabin crew staff. If an airline can get this part right, passengers will not only come back to them in the future, they will also recommend them to other would be passengers.

Organisational skills
Cabin crew staff must be organised both in their personal lives and their work lives. You will need to keep an organised diary to make sure you are available to meet your flying roster and you will also have to work in an organised manner before, during and after the flight. You will have check-lists to follow pre-flight and you will have certain procedures to follow during the flight. Being organised is all part and parcel of being a competent cabin crew member.

Numerical competence
Cabin crew need to be competent in the use of basic arithmetic. During the flight you will need to work with money when selling duty free goods and refreshments. You will also have to have an understanding of currency rates and conversions. Whilst you do not need to be a mathematician to become cabin crew, you should have a good basic understanding of addition, subtraction, multiplication and division.

Being a role model for the airline
This attribute is very similar to customer service skills. The airline wants you to promote them in the best possible light. Therefore, how you behave whilst at work, and also whilst away from work, are very important.

Excellent communication skills
Cabin crew have to be able to communicate with the following groups of people:

- Cockpit crew

- Passengers

- Other cabin crew team members

- Airport staff and representatives

Of course, there will be other people they will have to communicate with during their career; however, the above four groups are the main people they will come in to contact with during their day-to-day duties. Their communication skills must be excellent. Let's assume that there's a safety issue with the aircraft during the flight and you are required to communicate a safety message to the passengers using the public address (PA) system. It is essential that you remain calm and communicate the message in a confident and concise manner. If the passengers detect any hint of stress or concern in your voice, they will become agitated.

Of course, there are many other qualities required to become cabin crew; however, the above key attributes form the basis of the role. Before you attend the assessments and the interview make sure you learn them, understand them and be able to provide evidence of where you have already performed each one in a previous role.

Let's now take a look ten crucial tips that are designed to help you prepare fully for the selection process.

CHAPTER THREE
THE TOP IO INSIDER TIPS AND ADVICE

In this section of the guide we will provide you with ten important tips that will go a long way to helping you pass the selection process.

TIP 1 - EFFECTIVE COMMUNICATION SKILLS

Good communication skills are essential to the role of a cabin crew member.

Although the job is glamorous it is still customer focused and you will need to demonstrate that you have the ability to communicate effectively at all times.

Try to think of an occasion when somebody has annoyed you. How did you react? Do you have the ability to stay calm

in a confrontational situation? Of course, everybody feels uncomfortable when faced with a confrontational person, but it is your ability to defuse these situations that will set you apart from the rest of the candidates.

TIP 2 - KNOW HOW TO COMPLETE THE APPLICATION FORM CORRECTLY

Over 90% of candidates fail at the application form stage, usually due to a number of elements.

In the majority of cases, candidates fail to demonstrate that they have the right customer service skills to become a cabin crew member. Remember during the introduction section, we mentioned the importance of quality customer service and how it can affect an airline's profits? That is why it is so important that you take your time when answering these questions and structure your application form responses in an effective manner.

Even if you have no, or very little, experience of customer service skills, this should not stand in your way. Understanding the importance of it and being able to apply it throughout the selection process is far more important. Just because somebody has worked in a customer focused environment for many years, does not automatically mean they are good at providing it. Before completing your application form, read our section entitled 'The application form' for a detailed explanation on how to tackle the questions.

TIP 3 - CHOOSE THE RIGHT AIRLINE

Part of the advice we give you within this information guide is to learn as much information as possible about the airline

you are applying to join. If you decide that you want to apply for a number of airlines all in one go, you might not be able to give each application the preparation it deserves.

By demonstrating at the interview that you have researched their airline thoroughly, you show a higher level of commitment and you also demonstrate that you are committed to working with them. The mistake too many people make is that they focus their efforts on just 'becoming' a cabin crew member, when they should really be focusing their efforts on becoming a cabin crew member with 'x airline'.

Try to imagine yourself as one of the recruitment staff. You are presented with two candidates to choose from. They have both passed all of the assessments and would be good for your airline. One has applied for four different airlines and the other has only applied for yours. Which one would you choose?

TIP 4 - KNOW HOW TO HANDLE COMPLAINTS EFFECTIVELY

It is an unfortunate fact that on most flights cabin crew staff encounter complaints.

Part of the job is knowing how to deal with them correctly. If a flight is delayed, passengers are far more likely to complain about trivial things which they wouldn't normally bother about.

There are a whole host of reasons why people complain during a flight, but the fact is you need to know how to deal with them effectively and efficiently.

Try to imagine being on your way to the airport for a scheduled flight when your car breaks down. Eventually, road assistance arrives and repairs your car but already you are late for work.

Eventually you arrive at work and board the flight ready to commence your duties.

Obviously, you are not going to be as calm as normal following situations like this, but you will still have to provide a high level of customer service. The passengers do not care that you have just broken down and were nearly late for work as a result.

It is your ability to perform in situations like these that will set you apart from the rest of the candidates.

TIP 5 - KNOW WHAT TO WEAR FOR YOUR INTERVIEW

'You only get one chance to make a first impression.'

Such a true statement and one that you should keep at the forefront of your mind at all times during the selection process.

When you walk down the High Street of your local town, you will see people from different walks of life. We all form opinions of people without even talking to them, just judging them on their appearance and what clothes they are wearing.

It is only natural the interview panel will form an opinion of you as soon as they see you, so you will need to create the right impression immediately. Whilst you will probably have a good idea on what to wear, how to apply your make up if you wear it, and how to present yourself, you should still take the time to re-assess your appearance.

TIP 6 - CREATE AN EFFECTIVE INTRODUCTION

During the actual interview day, you will be required to introduce yourself to the rest of the candidates and the

selection staff.

This is done for a number of reasons. One of them is to allow the recruitment staff to see how confident you are and how well you present yourself and, secondly, it acts as an effective ice breaker.

Everybody will be nervous during the interview, that's a fact. But you still need to create a good impression right from the offset. The airline recruitment staff will be watching you and assessing your abilities right from the word go.

It is important that you write down and practice your introduction beforehand. Try standing up and saying your prepared introduction in front of your friends or relatives and you will see how difficult it can be. However, the more times you practice it, the better you will become at putting yourself across in a positive and confident manner.

Within this guide we have provided you with a sample introduction to help you get started.

TIP 7 - UNDERSTAND TEAM WORK

What does the term 'teamwork' actually mean? Here's a good explanation:

'Working as part of a group in which there is a shared goal. In order to achieve this, different members of the team take on different roles.'

When you are working as cabin crew, it is vital that you are capable of working as an effective team member. If you are ever placed in an emergency situation, then you will need to be able to work closely as a team to overcome any problems and make sure that all safety precautions and procedures are followed.

Are you able to create a rapport with any team you work with?

Can you bring something valuable to that team?

Do you make an effort to mix with the team and do you involve others?

During the selection process, you will be assessed in a team environment. You may be asked to take part in a group discussion and you'll be monitored in relation to how you react to certain situations and scenarios. Throughout this guide we will show you how to work effectively in a team environment.

TIP 8 - RESEARCH THE AIRLINE THOROUGHLY

Many people do not spend enough time researching their chosen airline. Then, when it comes to the interview, they fail to answer specific airline related questions effectively, and end up failing the whole process. You will be asked questions about the airline, how it operates, where they fly to and other important facts that you need to know as a cabin crew member.

This is no different to any other interview that you attend. The first and most important topic to research is the company and the role you are applying for.

There are a number of places that you can find relevant information about the airline you are applying for which we will discuss later on in the guide.

Now try to imagine what it must be like for those people who apply for 4 or 5 airlines at a time. Can they give sufficient preparation time to each one? Probably not.

Within the guide, we have provided you with a template that

contains all of the areas you should research. Make sure you research them thoroughly, and remember – knowledge is power, is confidence!

TIP 9 - KNOW THE INTERVIEW QUESTIONS

Imagine being told the type of questions that you will be asked prior to going into your interview. We will give you those questions.

We have spent hours talking to current serving cabin crew staff, recruitment staff and applicants who have failed the process, in order to obtain as many interview questions as possible.

We have also spent the time researching how to effectively answer those questions, so you don't have to. Read the 'Interview' section of this guide thoroughly, paying particular attention to the sample responses. Then, use the provided template to create your own personal and individual responses to the questions provided.

This will involve quite a lot of work but it will help you to get in the right frame of mind for the interview.

Then, to help you prepare fully, arrange a mock interview with a friend or relative. Get them to ask you various interview questions and spend time practicing the answers.

Try to choose someone who will give you constructive feedback as opposed to someone who will only tell you what you want to hear.

TIP 10 - AND FINALLY – DON'T GIVE UP!

Too many people give up at the first attempt. Yes, it is disheartening when you fail things in life but never give up. There have been many examples of people eventually succeeding at the 6th attempt, or even more. The key is to keep learning and improving your skills.

'If you always do what you've always done - you'll always get what you've always got!'

If you fail something in life, look upon it as an opportunity for improvement.

Where did you go wrong?

What can you do next time to improve?

Did you ask for feedback?

Can you learn from others?

Are you prepared to learn from your mistakes?

If you want something so bad then you can get it.

Sometimes it takes people years to get where they want to be. But by staying focused, motivated and driven, you can be what you want.

Now let's take a look at the application form and how you can complete it to ensure success.

CHAPTER FOUR

HOW TO COMPLETE THE APPLICATION FORM

INTRODUCTION

Around 95% of applicants fail this important stage which is usually due to a lack of preparation.

Each airline application form will vary slightly, but within this section we have provided you with insider tips and advice on how to complete it correctly.

TIP 1 - READ IT FIRST

Before you complete the application form, READ all of the sections, advice and guidance first, at least twice, to see

what is required. For example, at the top of the application form, or within the guidance notes, it may ask for a particular colour of ink. Having said that, the vast majority of application forms nowadays have to be completed online.

It is surprising how many people fail to follow simple instructions when completing the form. If you do not complete the application form as requested, then this shows an inability to follow simple instructions – an asset that is vital to the role of a cabin crew member.

TIP 2 - PRACTICE FIRST

Make sure you photocopy the application form and practice first. You are certain to make mistakes the first time round so it is wise to practice and write down your answers before completing your submission.

The application form may also provide you with boxes in which to complete your responses. Make sure you keep your answers within these boxes, unless specifically instructed otherwise.

TIP 3 - PERSONAL DETAILS

Within the application form, it will ask you to complete your personal details. This section is relatively straight forward, but some airlines ask you to complete it as shown on your passport.

Make sure you cross reference your passport and complete the details as shown, if required to do so.

TIP 4 - HEIGHT AND WEIGHT

Again, some airline application forms may vary, but you may find them asking you for your height and weight details. Please remember that this will be checked later on if you make it through to the preceding stages, so make sure that you complete it honestly.

There have been cases where candidates put down a weight less than they actually are, in a hope that they will shed the extra pounds in time for the next stage, only to find that they cannot achieve this.

We advise you to be honest when completing all sections of the application form. You may also be asked about tattoos and body piercing. Most airlines will not accept visible tattoos and only one earring per ear, but check first with the airline that you are applying for.

TIP 5 - PERSONAL QUALITIES

Within the application form, you will normally be asked to complete a section that relates to your personal qualities and attributes. The question may read:

"What qualities do you have that will make you a successful cabin crew member?"

Remember in the 'QUALITIES AND ATTRIBUTES' section we discussed some of these, and how important they are. When answering this section of the application form, it is important to let the panel know you have these skills. A sample answer to this question might be:

"I am an enthusiastic, loyal and resilient person who takes great pride in my appearance. Having previously

worked in a customer focused environment I fully understand the needs of others and believe my patience is a valuable asset in situations where others require my assistance. I thrive in any team environment and always try to use my excellent communication skills to listen to what others have to say whilst making valuable contributions myself. I have a friendly and caring personality which enables me to be supportive of my colleagues, and I always treat everybody as an individual"

TIP 5 - PERSONAL QUALITIES (CONTINUED)

Now, attempt to create your own response to this question based around your own personal qualities and attributes. Don't forget to consider the following keywords in your response:

KEY WORDS: Confident, enthusiastic, loyal, resilient, pride in my appearance, customer skills, needs of others, patient, helping others, considerate, team player, team environment, friendly and caring, excellent communication skills, listen, valuable contributions, supportive, capable of working under pressure, sense of humour, organised, mature.

TIP 6 - CUSTOMER SERVICE RESPONSE

Within the application form you may also be asked to complete a section in relation to customer service and where you have demonstrated this in a previous or current role.

The question may be posed in a manner similar to the following:

"Give an example of where you have provided excellent customer service."

Of course, each and every one of us has different work experiences that we can draw from, but this an extremely important section of the application form and it is important that you demonstrate the required qualities here.

The following is an example of the type of response the panel are seeking. Read the sample answer first and then decide how it made you feel. Does it make you feel that the person has demonstrated care and empathy for the customer's situation and was it resolved to a satisfactory conclusion?

Your customer service example is important and it could be the difference between making or not making it through to the next stage. Make sure you take your time when preparing your response. Again, take the time to construct your own, individual response but first read our example response.

TIP 6 - CUSTOMER SERVICE RESPONSE

"Whilst working as a sales representative for my current employer, I received a telephone call from an unhappy customer. Whilst listening to his concerns, I could sense that he was beginning to regret placing an order with our company. Before talking to him about the situation, I tried to realise how stressful it must be for him to be in this situation. I tried to think about what I could do to help reduce his worries and resolve the situation to his satisfaction. I informed him that I fully understood his concerns and I reassured him that I would do everything possible to help him. As soon as I told him this I could sense how thrilled he was to know that I would be helping him. I immediately dispatched

another order whilst on the phone to him, making sure that the order would be delivered that same day. I also told him that I would call him later that day to make sure he was happy with the new order.

Later that day, I telephoned the gentleman to check everything was to his satisfaction. The sound in his voice was very rewarding and I realised that with just a little help I had made such a difference to his day, making him feel like a valued customer."

FURTHER APPLICATION FORM QUESTIONS

As previously stated, each airline will vary in type of responses you are required to submit. On the following pages we have provided you with further examples, including responses.

"Detail all customer service experience which you feel would benefit your application."

Once again, the question relates directly to your customer service experience.

Some airlines require you to have a minimum of six months experience in a customer-based environment. This can be any type of customer experience, whether it be working in a shop, hotel, restaurant, or even answering the phone to customers or clients.

On the following page we have provided a sample response to this type of question.

As a starting point, you may find it helpful to write down your customer service experience before actually committing to a response. You'll be surprised at what experience you will have and how it can be adapted to fit the question. Once you

have read our example response on the following page, use
a blank sheet of paper to structure your own.

FURTHER APPLICATION FORM QUESTIONS - EXAMPLE

"Detail all customer service experience which you feel would benefit your application."

"In my current position as the manager of a restaurant, I am required to deliver excellent customer service, which includes the welcoming of customers, dealing with any complaints or queries, managing and leading the team to ensure we exceed the customers' expectations, providing a fast and efficient service and ensuring the team presents a highly professional image that represents the standards set by the restaurant.

Prior to my current position, I worked as a customer service representative, responsible for answering calls and dealing with queries and complaints about the service.

I was often confronted with unhappy customers and part of my role was to defuse confrontational situations and provide a resolution that the customers were happy with.

The best part of the job was having the ability to sort out the customers' problems in a satisfactory manner, making them feel that the company genuinely cared about their complaint or query."

"Having applied for the position of cabin crew, you are obviously interested in travel and people. What other reasons do you have for applying?"

This type of question is designed to assess the reasons why you want to become cabin crew. When responding to questions of this nature avoid talking about the glamorous side of the job or the fact that the image of cabin crew appeals to you.

Instead you should concentrate on the following areas:

- The reputation the airline has (providing it is positive);

- You enjoy working in a challenging role;

- The varied roster or shift system;

- Working in a customer-based role;

- Providing a high level of service.

On the following page we have provided a sample response to this type of question. Take the time to read the response before using a blank sheet of paper to construct your own individual response. Remember to be positive and enthusiastic in your reply.

"Having applied for the position of cabin crew, you are obviously interested in travel and people. What other reasons do you have for applying?"

"I have always had the ambition of becoming a cabin crew member from an early age, and now that I have the relevant customer service skills, I am ready to pursue my ambition. Other reasons for my application include the fact that I enjoy working in a customer-focused environment and thrive on the challenges that such a career brings. There is no better feeling

than successfully resolving issues for customers and I believe I would enjoy the responsibilities that a cabin crew member has.

I personally set myself high standards and would enjoy working for an airline that expects the same from its staff. I love working in a team environment where everybody pulls together to achieve a common goal.

I am the type of person who works well under pressure and would feel that the role of a cabin crew member would be suited to my qualities and attributes.

Finally, after researching the airline, I have been impressed by the high level of service it offers and the reputation that it has successfully built so far. I would like to be a part of that team and would work hard to ensure the current standards are maintained."

"Why are you interested in working for this airline?"

Remember the Top 10 Insider Tips and Advice, in particular Tip 8? - 'Research the airline thoroughly'. This is one of the reasons why you need to follow Tip 8. The only way that you can effectively answer this question is to research the airline.

When answering this type of question, try to include any success stories the airline might have achieved in recent times.

Areas that you should not include in your response relate to leave, salary, uniform, subsidised travel and holidays etc.

Focus on the facts about the airline and try to demonstrate that you have taken the time to look into the way it operates. Maybe you have flown with them before and had a good experience as a customer?

There now follows a sample response to this type of question. Read it thoroughly before using a blank sheet of paper to construct your own.

"Why are you interested in working for this airline?"

"There are a number of reasons why I would like to work for this airline. The first and foremost reason is the reputation the airline has.

I would like to work for an airline that sets high standards and takes a pride in the service it offers. I have been impressed by the developments this airline is currently in the process of implementing, which will mean improvements to check-in, baggage handling, on-board seating allocation, airport lounges and aircraft boarding. I believe it demonstrates a commitment to a continuing high level of customer service, and I would like to be a part of that team.

Because the airline is continuously improving, it is likely to mean there will be exciting and challenging times ahead, which appeals to me. I have also been impressed by the on-going development and training that is available through specialist courses provided by the airline, which would help me to maintain a high standard throughout my career, if I am to be successful.

Finally, I recently had the pleasure of travelling with the airline whilst on holiday. The cabin crew were exceptional in their professionalism and high level of service, which makes the airline an even more appealing one to work for."

"Describe one specific time during your working career when you have had to think quickly under

pressure in order to address a situation that required immediate action. What prompted you to try that approach and what was the result?"

This type of question has been designed to assess your ability to work quickly under pressure whilst having the confidence to take action when necessary.

Try to think of an example when you have had to work quickly under pressure to prevent a situation from deteriorating. Make sure you give the reasons why you took that particular action and explain the result. You may also wish to say, at the end of your response, what you learned from your experience.

On the following page we have provided you with a sample response to give you some ideas to help you create your own.

The response we have provided explains a situation where a member of staff is following a set routine which he/she has been given during training (something you will be required to do as a cabin crew member).

It also emphasises the need for ensuring everyone was safe throughout the incident, including an explanation for why it was necessary to remain calm (again, something you will have to do whilst working as a cabin crew member).

"Describe one specific time during your working career when you have had to think quickly under pressure in order to address a situation that required immediate action. What prompted you to try that approach and what was the result?"

"Whilst working for my current employer as a shop sales assistant, I was confronted with an emergency situation during a busy Saturday morning. I was stock-

taking in the store room which is located on the 3rd floor of the store. Whilst working, I suddenly began to smell a strong burning smell but could not tell where it was coming from.

I immediately began to follow the procedures given during my staff induction training and raised the alarm by breaking the alarm call point located at the store room exit. I walked calmly out of the store room, but noticed that all the customers were ignoring the alarm and continuing to shop.

I immediately shouted, in a calm but raised voice, for everyone to leave the shop, via the nearest stairway exit, due to an incident. I re-emphasised the importance that people should not use the lifts. People began to leave via the stairway and I went over to the till area and called the Fire Brigade before making my way out via the stairs.

On the way down, I calmly informed other members of staff that there was an incident and that we should leave the shop and await the arrival of the Fire Brigade.

When we got outside, a roll-call of all members of staff was taken. The Fire Brigade soon arrived and I informed them of the location of the store room and the reason that the alarm had been raised. Following their investigation, it was found that an electrical socket had overheated and was smouldering at the rear of the store room.

The reason that I took this action was that I am required to follow the training provided during my staff induction. Although I was effectively evacuating the whole of the store and losing the company money,

the safety of the customers and other staff members was paramount. I did everything in a calm manner. I needed to remain calm throughout so that the customers would not panic whilst evacuating. If they were to panic, then injury could have occurred whilst they were leaving the shop via the stairs.

The end result was that everybody was accounted for and there were no injuries. Also, the possibility of a major fi re was averted because the Fire Brigade were called quickly and were, therefore, able to deal with the fi re before it got out of hand."

"Describe one specific time during your working career when you had to convey an unpopular decision to an individual or group. How did you approach that person or group? How did you deal with the situation? Was the situation resolved?"

This type of question is designed to assess your ability to deal with difficult situations in an assertive manner.

Giving unpopular news or constructive feedback is difficult, even for the most confident of people.

When working as a cabin crew member you will sometimes be dealing with passengers who are rude and confrontational. You will be required to deal with these situations and sometimes give passengers unwelcome news.

Being able to do this in an effective manner is quite a skill, and the airline recruitment staff want to see you have the potential to do this in a real life situation.

There now follows a sample response to this type of question. Read it carefully before structuring your own response using

a blank sheet of paper.

"Describe one specific time during your working career when you had to convey an unpopular decision to an individual or group. How did you approach that person or group? How did you deal with the situation? Was the situation resolved?"

"Whilst working in my current position as a hotel receptionist, I was confronted with a situation where our central reservation booking system had mistakenly double booked two sets of couples.

The guests arrived at the hotel at midday ready to check in for the weekend. I commenced the checking-in procedure and it was then that I realised the rooms had already been taken. In addition to this problem, we were fully booked and had no spare rooms to offer them as an alternative.

I decided that the best way to approach the problem was to be honest with them and tell them about the mistake that we had made. However, I felt that the best place to break the news was in a quiet room away from the reception area. I asked my colleague to take over the reception desk and I asked the guests to follow me to a conference room, which was out of the way.

I sat them down and began to explain what had happened in a calm and apologetic manner. Naturally, they were annoyed and disappointed with the situation. I reassured them that we would do everything in our power to resolve the issue.

I then informed them that I would need a short amount of time to resolve the issue and asked them

to remain in the bar area where they would be served complimentary drinks and food. I then went away to speak to the duty manager and to request permission to seek alternative accommodation which the hotel would pay for. I returned to the group and explained that the hotel would try to arrange other accommodation in the area, to an equal or higher standard than that which they had booked with us. I explained that we would refund their payment in full as well as paying for the new hotel room, as compensation for the inconvenience caused.

They agreed to this and appeared to be happy with the level of service I was offering them. The situation was eventually resolved after I had managed to find alternative accommodation for the guests in the local area. The following week, I followed up with a letter to both couples further apologising and offering them a discounted rate for any future visits. Since then, one of the couples has returned to the hotel and used our services."

"Please supply any additional information which you feel might benefit your application."

This type of question serves one purpose – the opportunity for you to sell yourself. The type of response you provide will be very much dependant on your own experiences, personality and attributes. If you are given the opportunity to supply additional information, then you should do. Within your response, summarise your skills, experience and attributes whilst reiterating the reasons why you want to join their team.

Always make sure you end on a positive note! There now follows a sample response to this type of question. Read the

response before using the template on the preceding page to design your own.

Finally, before submitting your application, make sure you read each response and check for mistakes, grammar and punctuation. Remember that you are trying to create a professional image.

"Please supply any additional information which you feel might benefit your application."

"I have been working hard to research both the role that I am applying for and the airline I have chosen to join. I have taken my application seriously and have studied the qualities and attributes that are required of a competent cabin crew member and I believe I would be a valuable asset to your team.

My experience and skills already gained in my working life will stand me in good stead to become a professional, reliable and dedicated employee. Thank you for taking the time to read my application."

Now move on to the next section of the guide, the team assessments.

CHAPTER FIVE

THE ASSESSMENT DAY

INTRODUCTION

For the majority of airlines, the assessment day will consist of the following:

- Introduction;
- Written tests;
- Team assessments.

The assessment day normally comes after the application form stage so if you have progressed this far, well done! At the beginning of the day, the airline recruitment staff will ask each candidate to introduce themselves to them and the other members of the group.

This is the first chance they will get to see you and what you are about. It is your first opportunity to create a positive impact, so you need to ensure you prepare your introduction in advance, and rehearse it. Many candidates will not prepare an introduction or will not be ready for it, so having one prepared beforehand is a good thing.

The areas that you should try to cover during your introduction are as follows:

Your name, where you live, your current or previous occupation, interests, hobbies and ambitions, and what you have achieved.

YOUR INTRODUCTION

Take a look at the following sample introduction.

"Good morning everybody, it's a real pleasure to meet you all! My name is Mark and I'm 25 years old. My current job is as a hotel porter for a reputable leisure industry chain which I absolutely love. I get great satisfaction from helping our guests and making their stay the more enjoyable. The tips are also quite good too!

At the moment I am living in Worcester, but if I am successful in my ambition to become a cabin crew member with this airline, I will be relocating to xxxx. Recently, I raised £500 for a local charity by walking up and down the hotel stairs 50 times without stopping. There are 15 floors to the building and after the 10th time I wish I would have used the lift instead!

I am so happy to be here today, and to have been given the opportunity of fulfilling a life-long dream

of becoming cabin crew. I can't wait to meet you all and look forward to talking to so many great people, thanks."

This introduction is extremely effective. The introduction is positive and, therefore, should be portrayed in this manner. He talks about a charity event where he raised money for a good cause. He also uses a small amount of humour which works very well.

He talks about his current role which is customer-focused and that he enjoys it very much. Remember, never to put down or criticise your employer. This is not a good thing to do and it will be frowned upon.

When it is your turn to stand up and introduce yourself, stand tall, be positive, enthusiastic and cheerful. Be genuinely glad to be at the assessment day and look forward to the whole process.

Using a blank sheet of paper, create your own introduction, based on your own personal circumstances.

WRITTEN TESTS

The majority of airlines will ask you to sit a general knowledge test and a mathematics test. These are usually multiple-choice in nature and the pass mark is approximately 70%.

Make sure you check with the airline first to confirm which tests you are required to sit.

MATHEMATICS TEST

The mathematics test includes basic forms of addition, subtraction, multiplication and division. The general

knowledge test is exactly that, a test of your general knowledge.

The most effective way to prepare for the mathematics test is to practice basic arithmetic questions.

As a cabin crew member, you will be required to perform basic mathematical sums during flights and when dealing with customers change.

On the following page we have provided you with a mathematics test to help you prepare. Write down your answers on a blank sheet of paper or use the answer sheet provided on the following page.

Allow yourself 10 minutes to complete the exercise.

Calculators are not permitted.

GOOD LUCK.

MATHEMATICAL CALCULATION TEST

This type of test is designed to test your basic arithmetic skills.

It will test your ability in relation to addition, subtraction, multiplication and division and is an ideal way of practising for psychometric tests. By practising these tests, you will find that your ability to work quickly and accurately under pressure will improve.

The use of a calculator is not permitted during these tests and you should not use one when attempting the following exercise. In each question a mathematical sum is given with one area missing. This missing area is the one you must identify as the answer.

For example:

5 + 10 = 15 - ?

Answer = 1,0,2,4,3

The answer to this question is 0.

Explanation: 5 +10 =15, so therefore 15-0=15.

MATHEMATICAL CALCULATION TEST - EXERCISE 1

1. 37 + ? = 95

2. 86 - ? = 32

3. ? − 104 = 210

4. 109 × ? = 218

5. 6 + 9 + 15 = 15 × ?

6. 34 + 13 − 4 = ? + 3

7. 35 ÷ ? = 10 + 7.5

8. 7 × ? = 28 × 3

9. 100 ÷ 4 = 67 - ?

10. 32 × 9 = 864 ÷ ?

11. 11 × ? = 265 − 144

12. 14 × 28 = ?

13. (4000 + 56) ÷ ? = 1014

14. (32 × 2) × 4 = 512 - ?

15. 2.5 × 3 = 37.5 ÷ ?

16. (8 ÷ 2) × 16 = 150 - ?

17. 87 − 1 = (45 − 2) × ?

18. (17 + 15) − 8 = ? × 3

19. (7 × 10) × 3 = ? × 6

20. (19 + 19) ÷ 19 = (? × 2) ÷ 2

ANSWERS TO EXERCISE 1

1. 58
   The quickest way to get to the answer is to subtract 37 from 95 which leaves 58.

2. 54
   Subtract 32 from 86 to be left with 54.

3. 314
   Add 210 to 104 to get 314.

4. 2
   Divide 218 by 109 to get the answer of 2.

5. 2
   6 + 9 + 15 = 30 so therefore 15 multiplied by 2 gives you 30.

6. 40
   34 + 13 = 47. Then subtract 4 to be left with 43.
   Therefore 40 + 3 gives you 43.

7. 2
   10 + 7.5 will give you 17.5; therefore 15 divided by 2 will give you 17.5.

8. 12
   28 × 3 will give you 84; therefore 7 × 12 will also give you 84.

9. 42
   100 divided by 4 will give you 25; therefore 67 - 25 will leave you with 42.

10. 3
    32 × 9 will give you 288. Now multiply 288 by 3 to get 864.

11. 11

265 - 164 gives you 121; therefore 11 multiplied by 11 will also give you 121.

12. 392

14 × 28 will give you 392.

13. 4

(4000 + 56) gives you 4056. Divide 4056 by the answer 1014 to get the answer 4.

14. 256

32 × 2 will give you 64. Then multiply 64 by 4 to get 256. 512 – 256 leaves you with 256.

15. 5

2.5 × 3 will give you 7.5, then 37.5 divided by 5 will leave you with 7.5

16. 86

8 divided by 2 will give you 4. Then multiply 4 by 16 to get 64. Then 150 subtract 86 will leave you with 64.

17. 2

87 – 1 will give you 86. Then, 45 – 2 will give you 43. Multiply 43 by 2 to reach 86.

18. 8

17 + 15 will give you 32. Subtract 8 from 32 to be left with 24. Then multiply 8 by 3 to be left with the same figure 24.

19. 35

7 × 10 will give you 70 which when multiplied by 3 will give you 210. Then 35 × 6 equals the same figure 210.

20. 2

19 + 19 will give you 38 which, when divided by 19, will give you 2. Then 2 × 2 will give you 4 which, when divided by 2, will give you the answer 2.

GENERAL KNOWLEDGE TEST

Some airlines will ask you to sit a general knowledge test as part of their selection process. The pass mark can vary but it is usually around the 70% mark. It is advised that you check with the airline that you are applying to join, to see whether they will require you to sit this type of test.

The type and nature of the questions that you will be asked during this test vary, however the general type of questions will be centred around current affairs, political issues, capitals, currencies and 'who's who' questions.

During your preparation for these tests, try to look at the following areas:

- Currency and currency conversions.
- Capitals of major cities.
- Airport locations and terminals.
- Countries.
- The 24 hour clock.
- Duty free allowances.
- Airline industry/time abbreviations – EU, UCT, BAA, GMT etc.

On the following page we have included a general knowledge test for you to practice, to become accustomed to the types of questions you may encounter.

GENERAL KNOWLEDGE TEST

Allow yourself 5 minutes to complete the following exercise:

1. What is the capital of America?

2. Name a state in America beginning with 'W'.

3. In relation to time, what do the initials GMT stand for?

4. What is the currency of Egypt?

5. What is the currency of Thailand?

6. What continent is Zambia in?

7. Which is the highest mountain in the world?

8. How many states are there in the USA?

9. Who is the current Deputy Prime Minister?

10. What is celebrated on the 4th of July in America?

11. What do the initials BAA stand for?

12. What are the names of the 2 terminals at London Gatwick?

13. Which motorway connects Stansted Airport to the M25 motorway?

14. What is the currency of Spain?

15. How many engines does a Boeing 747 have?

ANSWERS TO GENERAL KNOWLEDGE TEST

1. Washington.

2. Washington, West Virginia, Wisconsin or Wyoming.

3. Greenwich Mean Time.

4. Egyptian Pound.

5. Baht.

6. Southern Africa.

7. Mount Everest.

8. 50.

9. Nick Clegg.

10. Independence Day.

11. The British Aviation Authority.

12. North and South Terminals.

13. The M11.

14. The Euro.

15. 4.

THE TEAM ASSESSMENTS

Team assessments form another integral part of the cabin crew selection process. The airline recruitment staff will be looking for candidates to demonstrate specific qualities throughout the team assessment. Many employers use team assessments to test a candidate's performance and ability, and they are a very good indicator of someone's confidence, motivation and enthusiasm. The team assessment stage will usually require you, and a number of other potential candidates, to come up with a solution to a problem, all within a specific time frame. During the assessment, you will be given a scenario to deal with and you'll have to decide amongst yourselves the most appropriate method of resolving the issue.

During the assessment, you will often see candidates fighting to get their views across. Many candidates will start talking over the top of other people, but this is not the best way to approach the assessment. This is where you will have the opportunity to demonstrate you have the right qualities to work as part of a team and come up with answers to problems. The solution or answer that the team come up with doesn't have to be the right one. However, the panel are looking for you come up with a logical solution.

AN EXPLANATION

The number of candidates taking part in the team assessment will vary from airline to airline, but to give you an idea, there are usually about a dozen.

At the beginning of the team assessment, you will be provided with a brief and you will then be given a set time in order to come up with a solution. Throughout the team assessment,

you will have a member of the airline recruitment staff monitoring the session and scoring each of you individually.

The important thing to remember, during the team assessment, is how you present yourself. Yes, it is good to provide a solution to the problem, but there is so much more to the assessment than problem solving. On the following page we have provided you with some of the key areas that you will tested on during the assessment. Take a look at each assessable area before moving onto the sample exercises.

HOW TO SCORE POSITIVELY DURING THE TEAM ASSESSMENTS

AREA NUMBER 1 – INVOLVING OTHERS

During the assessment, you must try to involve other people. If during the assessment, you notice a person who is not getting involved or saying anything, try to involve them. Ask them a question such as – "What do you think we should do?". You will receive positive marks for involving others during the assessment.

AREA NUMBER 2 – COMMUNICATION SKILLS

Use effective listening skills throughout the assessment, both verbal and nonverbal. Make sure you listen to what other people are saying and use facial expressions and actions to indicate that you are doing so.

AREA NUMBER 3 – POSITIVE TEAMWORKING

During the assessment, make an effort to get on with the group. Smile, be positive and show that you have the ability to work effectively in a team environment.

Don't try to show off or gain points by doing things on your own. Yes, come up with positive solutions, but involve the group and get involved with them.

AREA NUMBER 4 – MAKING POSITIVE CONTRIBUTIONS

Try to think of positive solutions to the problem. Remember that you don't have to necessarily solve the problem totally, but do try to come up with a logical solution and one that would work.

If somebody doesn't agree with your solution, be willing to change or accept that maybe there is a better idea.

AREA 5 – PROVIDE POSITIVE FEEDBACK

If somebody comes up with a good idea during the assessment, tell them so. Provide encouragement to the group by saying phrases such as – "I think that's a great idea, that would work", or "Yes, I think that would work, because…"

AREA 6 – EFFECTIVE BODY LANGUAGE

Throughout the assessment, have a positive body language. If you are sat down, do not slouch. Instead, sit upright and be enthusiastic about getting involved with the group. Be positive in your nature, smile and laugh where appropriate.

AREA 7 – BUILD ON IDEAS TO SOLVE THE PROBLEM

If a member of the group offers a solution, try to build on it. Don't dismiss people's ideas just because you don't agree with them. Look for ways to see if they will work.

SAMPLE ASSESSMENTS

On the following page we have provided a sample team assessment exercise to help you prepare. Please note that airlines use a variety of different scenarios and this is not the exact scenario that you will be presented with on the day. It is provided as a practice aid only.

Remember that It is not the scenario that is important but, rather, how you deal with it effectively in the team environment. If you do not take part in the team assessments you are guaranteed to fail. Make sure you get involved!

Take a look at the sample exercise on the following page. Once you have read it, try to look at ways in which you could solve the problem. On the page after, we have provided you with an indicator sheet to help you take notes in relation to some of the key areas you should be looking to demonstrate.

SAMPLE TEAM ASSESSMENT – EXERCISE 1

TEAM BRIEFING

An important guest will be arriving the following day at your airline's headquarters and he has requested a selection of food to be available. He is a major shareholder within the company.

Your task is to discuss amongst yourselves what would be the most appropriate choice of food and refreshments from the list below.

Please indicate why you chose your selection:

LIST

- Roast Dinner;

- Fish and Chips;

- A selection of cold meats, salads, vegetables and fruit;

- A hot buffet including selection of wines and non-alcoholic drinks.

SAMPLE TEAM ASSESSMENT – EXERCISE 1 INDICATOR SHEET

Area number 1 – Involving others

Area number 2 – Communication skills

Area number 3 – Positive teamworking

Area number 4 – Making positive contributions

Area 5 – Provide positive feedback

Area 6 – Effective body language

Area 7 – Build on ideas to solve the problem

SAMPLE TEAM ASSESSMENT – EXERCISE 2

TEAM BRIEFING

The Chief Executive of the airline has asked your team to arrange the entertainment at the forthcoming Christmas Party.

You have a budget of £4,000 and it is your task to provide the entertainment from the list below.

Please state why you have chosen your particular selection:

- Dave's Disco – price £1,200;

- A 'Hot Chocolate' tribute band – price £2,900;

- A 'Robbie Williams' tribute band – price £2,500;

- A comedian – price £500;

- A 70's funk band – price £2,200.

SAMPLE TEAM ASSESSMENT – EXERCISE 2 INDICATOR SHEET

Area number 1 – Involving others

Area number 2 – Communication skills

Area number 3 – Positive teamworking

Area number 4 – Making positive contributions

Area 5 – Provide positive feedback

Area 6 – Effective body language

Area 7 – Build on ideas to solve the problem

SOME FINAL ADVICE

During the assessment, remember to focus on the relevant areas that you are trying to demonstrate. Don't become too engrossed in providing a good solution to the problem or scenario. Keep your eye on the main objective.

If a member of the team is controlling the situation, talking too much and not allowing others to talk, tell them politely that you would like to talk. If you are not confident enough to do this, then try putting your hand up.

Remember to involve others in the group.

Don't get involved in an argument, even if somebody annoys you.

Keep an eye on the time. You will only have a set amount of time to provide a solution.

Remember – you will score more points for involving others and providing positive feedback than you will for 'controlling' the team and talking over everybody.

As hard as it may be, try to enjoy the assessment.

CHAPTER SIX
THE CABIN CREW INTERVIEW

ABOUT THE CABIN CREW INTERVIEW

During the selection process for becoming cabin crew you will have to undertake at least one interview. This will usually form part of the main assessment day; however, many airlines will also invite you back for a further second interview if you pass the assessment day. The questions in this guide will help you prepare for both sets of interviews and I would urge you to use the same preparation strategy for each interview. In this section we will look at the cabin crew interview and what it involves.

The cabin crew selection panel are highly experienced in being able to determine who are the right people for the job. Therefore, it is vitally important that you prepare well for this stage. The interview panel will normally consist of 2-3 people,

with one person being a senior member of the cabin crew training team for that particular airline. There may also me a member of the human resources department sitting on the panel to ensure the interview is conducted in a fair manner.

In order to pass the interview you will need to provide the selection panel with evidence of where you meet the assessable qualities. Although I will be covering the scoring criteria in the next section of the guide, I want you to have the word EVIDENCE at the forefront of your mind at all times during your preparation. In order to score highly during the interview you need to come up with examples of where you have already demonstrated the key assessable qualities in a previous job or career. If you do this, you will be more likely to succeed during the interview.

The interview panel will be assessing you on the following key areas:

- Your knowledge of the airline you are applying to join
- Your knowledge of the role of cabin crew
- What qualities and expertise you can bring to the role
- The experiences you have that match the assessable qualities
- Your personal appearance and presentation
- Your communication skills
- Your levels of confidence
- Whether or not you meet the qualities discussed in the previous section of this guide.

So, in order to prepare fully for the above assessable areas, you need to direct your pre-interview preparation on the following key areas:

RESEARCH

Research, in terms of the role you are applying for and the particular airline you are hoping to join, is essential. During the interview, you are likely to be asked questions relating to the following areas:

- **What you know about the role of a cabin crew member.**
  You should study the role of air cabin crew in detail and think carefully about what it involves. You should also think about the positive sides of the job and also the negatives.

- **The reasons for applying and why you want to join this particular airline.**
  This is important because many applicants simply want to become cabin crew and they do not care which airline it is with. My advice is to ensure that you have a good reason for wanting to join their airline. My motto has always been:

Airline first, cabin crew second!

- **What you know about their airline.**
  The most effective way to find out this information is to go to the website of the airline you wish to join. From the website you will be able to find out as much information as possible about what they do, where they fly to and from and also what their values are. In order to help you, here is a checklist of things you need to learn:

AIRLINE RESEARCH CHECKLIST

Research Topic	Done?
Who are the senior airline executives and the CEO?	
What aircraft do they operate?	
Where do they fly to and from?	
What are the main services offered?	
Have they won any awards?	
What is their customer charter?	
How do they protect the environment? NOTE: this is sometimes called corporate responsibility.	

What are the special
services or special
assistance do they offer
passengers?

How many people work
for the airline?

What is the airlines history
and heritage?

Where is the airlines head
office located?

What is new and current
within the airline?

Who, if anyone, does the
airline sponsor?

What was their latest
twitter post?

What was their latest
Facebook post?

The above checklist is an excellent starting pout to help you
get your research of the airline underway.

- **How you deal with specific situations in your working life and what you learn from them.**
  This is of particular importance and one area that may take you some time to prepare for. This is essentially where you will provide the panel with evidence of your previous experiences; such as, when you have provided excellent customer service, when you have dealt with a customer complaint and also when you have remained calm in a difficult and distressing situation.

When responding to **situational** interview questions I strongly recommend that you use the **S.T.A.R** method for constructing your responses. Here's an explanation of what it means:

When constructing your responses to the situational questions within this guide, create them using the following format:

S – situation

Start off by explaining what the situation was and who was involved.

T – task

Now move on and tell the panel what the task was that you were required to carry out or complete.

A – action

Then tell the interview panel what action you took and also what action other people took when trying to complete the task.

R – result

Finish off by telling the panel what the result was following your actions and the actions of the other people involved in the situation. Always try to ensure that the result is a positive one!

If you follow the above method for creating your responses to situational interview questions then your responses will be formulaic, concise and in a logical sequence. This will help you to gain higher scores in the assessable area of effective communication.

- **Challenges faced by the airline.**
  This can be a tricky one to answer; however, just by typing in the words "challenges faced by the airline industry" in to any one of the search engines you will be able to formulate you own views on this subject. To give you an idea of the different challenges at the time of writing, here are my thoughts:

  1. **The environmental impact of the airline industry and an airlines carbon footprint.**
     This is a challenge simply because the demand for air traffic is increasing and is set to continue. With more and more people wanting to fly it is a challenge for airlines to meet their targets.

  2. **The competition within the industry.**
     The competition is becoming fiercer with more airlines offering flights at cheaper prices. Attracting and retaining customers is getting harder. However, by offering customer excellent customer services they are far more likely to return and use the airline again in the future. This is how cabin crew can help the airline meet this challenge.

3. **The rising cost of fuel.**
   With the rising cost of fuel it is difficult for airlines to keep their costs down without passing on the added expense to their passengers.

Of course, the above 3 challenges are not the only ones facing the airline industry; however, they are a good starting point.

- **Your own personal qualities and attributes.**
  In order to prepare for question based around this topic I would urge you to think carefully about the role of cabin crew and also the qualities required to carry out the role competently. It is important that you have these qualities and attributes and be able to demonstrate them at interview.

- **Your strengths and weaknesses.**
  Only you will know what these are; however, the following are good strengths to have when applying for this type of job:

  - Resilience and confidence

  - Flexibility

  - Caring nature and attitude

  - Excellent team working skills

  - Empathy and understanding

  - Good communication skills

  - Personal pride in appearance

In terms of weaknesses, we all have them and anyone who says otherwise is not being honest. However, be careful what weaknesses you give. I have always

thought that this is a good weakness to give during the cabin crew interview:

"My weakness is that I detest lateness and on occasions in the past I have been known to be quite blunt and to tell people my thoughts whenever they are late for a meeting or appointment that we have pre-arranged. Because I am never late myself, I expect this of other people and my comments have sometimes been taken the wrong way. However, I am learning that not everyone has high standards in relation to punctuality and I try not to say anything to them."

The above response is quite a good one as it demonstrates to the panel that you are never late, something which is crucial to the role of cabin crew. Whatever weakness you decide to give, make sure you tell the panel that you are taking steps to improve on your weak areas.

- **Team-working skills**
  The interview panel will most certainly want to hear evidence of where you have worked effectively as part of a small team. Cabin crew are required to work with other team members to achieve a common goal. That goal is essentially to get the passengers to their destination on time whilst ensuring their safety and providing excellent customer service. Before you go to the interview I strongly advise that you are capable of providing examples of where you have worked effectively as part of a team. Here is a list of just some of the qualities required to work as an effective team member:

  - Good communicator

  - Good listening skills

- Understanding of others

- Able to focus on the end goal

- Being adaptable and flexible

- Supporting other team members

- Being aware of yours and the other team members strengths and weaknesses

- Hardworking and focused

- Professional and conscientious

- Open to feedback

Before you go to the cabin crew interview I recommend that you learn and understand the above list of team working qualities.

- **Respect and diversity**
  As cabin crew you will be required to work with and interact with people from all walks of life. It is absolutely crucial that you are capable of working with anyone, regardless of their age, sex, religious beliefs, background, sexual orientation, disabilities or otherwise.

Let's now take a look at a number of sample interview questions ad responses to help you prepare.

QUESTION NUMBER 1

Why do you want to become a cabin crew member?

You will, most probably, have already answered this question when completing the application form. If this is the case, have a look at your application form response prior to the interview to make sure you give an alternative answer and also that you do not contradict yourself the second time around.

When answering this question, concentrate on covering the following elements:

- The main reason why – your ambition.

- The suitability of your personal qualities and attributes.

- The positive aspects of the role – variety, flexibility, working with others, etc.

- Helping others/Customer care, etc.

We have provided you with a sample response to this type of question.

Once you have read our response, use it to construct your own using a blank sheet of paper.

QUESTION NUMBER 1 – SAMPLE RESPONSE

Why do you want to become a cabin crew member?

"This is something that I have always wanted to do. Ever since I flew on holiday as a child, I have aspired to a member of a cabin crew team.

Although I enjoy my current job, I would now like a career that is more challenging, varied and exciting.

I believe my own personal qualities would suit the role of a cabin crew member and I get great satisfaction from working in a team environment, where everybody is working towards the same goal.

I understand that delivering a high level of service to the customer is a priority in this industry, and this is something that I would enjoy doing."

KEY AREAS TO CONSIDER:

The main reason for wanting to become a cabin crew member:

- The positive aspects of the job.

- Working in a team environment.

- Providing a high standard of customer care.

QUESTION NUMBER 2

Why do you want to work for our airline?

Once again, you may have already answered this question during the application form stage. If this is the case, remember to check your answer first before attending the interview.

When answering this question, you must be positive about their airline. The main reason for the panel asking this question is that they want to know you have researched them thoroughly, and that you are serious about wanting to join them. Many candidates apply for many different airlines just because they want to become a cabin crew member. Wanting to join their particular airline is just as important as wanting to become a cabin crew member.

When answering this type of question, try to cover the following areas:

- Their reputation (providing it is positive).

- The quality of their product.

- The airlines ambitions and achievements.

- What they stand for.

Now, take a look at the sample response that follows before creating your own using a blank sheet of paper.

QUESTION NUMBER 2 – SAMPLE RESPONSE

Why do you want to work for our airline?

"Prior to attending the selection process, I researched a number of different airlines before deciding to apply for yours. I was impressed by the quality of service the

airline offers and I already know that it has an excellent reputation. Your customer service standards are high and the quality of training all cabin crew members receive is exceptional.

Having spoken to some of your existing employees, all of them were very happy in their work and stated that you are a very good employer. You are an exciting airline that has achieved much to date and I like the fact that you are always looking for innovative ways to improve and develop.

I would like to work for an airline that cares about its customers, which you do. If the customer is happy and their experience of flying with you is a good one, they are likely to come back again.

I would love to be a part of this team and believe the qualities I have will help it to continue to move forward and stay ahead of its competitors."

KEY AREAS TO CONSIDER:

- The airline's reputation.

- The quality of their product and what they stand for.

- The airline's ambitions and achievements.

QUESTION NUMBER 3

What makes you better than the next candidate and, therefore, why should we offer you the position?

This is another opportunity for you to sell yourself. This is quite a common question during interviews and the way you approach it should be in a positive manner.

The question is designed to assess your confidence and determine the type of qualities you have. Don't fall into the trap of answering this question in the same way that the majority of people do.

Many people will reply with a response along the following line:

"I am the best person for the job because this is something that I've always wanted to do. I am a hard worker who is enthusiastic and determined to be successful."

This type of response is not factual or unique in content. Try to focus your response on the job and how best you match it. The airline want to know that they'll look back in a years' time, and think that they are glad they employed you.

Take a look at our sample response before constructing your own using a blank sheet of paper.

QUESTION NUMBER 3 – SAMPLE RESPONSE

What makes you better than the next candidate and, therefore, why should we offer you the position?

"I have researched both the role that I am applying for, and your airline. Looking at the required skills of

the role and the type of person you are looking for, I believe I am the best person for the job.

I have a proven track record in delivering a high level of customer service and have experience in dealing with customer complaints. I have been on a number of training courses before and always ensure that I put in the required amount of work to successfully pass them to a high standard.

I am a confident and reliable person who works very well in a team environment. In my previous role as a restaurant manager, I often had to work to tight schedules and always remained calm when under pressure.

Finally, my personal circumstances are extremely flexible and, having studied the role of a cabin crew member, I understand the obligations and requirements in terms of availability. If successful, I promise that I won't let you down and I will work hard to make sure that I live up to expectations of the airline."

KEY AREAS TO CONSIDER:

- Your previous experience and how it relates to the role.

- Be positive, confident and upbeat in your response.

- Cover the key qualities and attributes and match them with your own experience.

QUESTION NUMBER 4

What are your weaknesses and what do you need to work on?

This is a classic interview question and can be quite difficult to answer for many people.

Those people who say they have no weaknesses are not telling the truth. We all have areas that we can improve on, but you need to be careful what you disclose when responding to this type of question.

For example, if you tell the panel that you are an awful time keeper you might as well leave the interview there and then! They will admire your honesty, but the role requires people who are punctual and are not going to be late for work.

The best way to prepare for this type of question is to write down all of your weaknesses. Once you have done that, pick one that you can turn into a positive. Take a look at the sample response that follows and see how we have turned the weakness around to our advantage.

Once you have read the response, use a blank sheet of paper to prepare your own response based on your own circumstances.

QUESTION NUMBER 4 – SAMPLE RESPONSE

What are your weaknesses and what do you need to work on?

"That's a difficult question to answer but I am aware of a weakness that I have. I tend to set myself high standards both personally and professionally.

The problem is, I sometimes expect it from other people, too. For example, I find it difficult to accept

it when people are late for an appointment that we have agreed.

In those situations, I need to learn to let it go over my head and just accept that everybody is different."

KEY AREAS TO CONSIDER:

- Be honest, but don't talk about any weaknesses you may have that are in relation to the job description.

- Turn your weakness into a positive.

- Say that you are working on your weakness.

- If you really cannot think of a weakness, tell them about one that you used to have.

QUESTION NUMBER 5

Describe a situation at work where you have had to be flexible.

Part of the cabin crew's role is to be flexible.

Part of the essential criteria for becoming a cabin crew member is that you are flexible. This means that you are flexible in terms of the roster and your availability.

In order for the airline to operate effectively, it needs people who do not want to work a normal 9 – 5 job. You may have to be at the airport for 3am in order to prepare for your flight at 5am. Are you flexible enough to do this?

Many cabin crew staff say that the most frustrating aspect of their job is the instability of the life and the roster changes. Obviously the airline want to know that this is not going to be a problem for you. Therefore, when responding to this type of question, you need to provide an example where you have already demonstrated commitment and flexibility to a previous or current role.

Read the sample response we have provided before using a blank sheet of paper to create your own response.

QUESTION NUMBER 5 – SAMPLE RESPONSE

Describe a situation at work where you have had to be flexible.

"Whilst working in my current role as a hairdresser, I was asked by my employer to work late every Saturday evening. The reason for this was that a number of clients could only make appointments between 6pm and 8pm on Saturday evenings. Although I usually go out on a Saturday night, I decided to agree to the

additional hours. The salon was doing well and was beginning to get a very good reputation. I wanted to help the salon provide a high level of service to its customers and understood that if I didn't work late on those evenings they would lose the custom.

Fortunately, 2 months on, another member of the team has volunteered to help me cover the Saturday evenings, so I now only have to work every other Saturday.

I fully understand that cabin crew members need to be flexible in terms of their roster and working hours. My personal life would allow for this and I believe it is a small sacrifice to pay for such a rewarding career. I can be relied upon to be flexible when required."

KEY AREAS TO CONSIDER:

- Demonstrate that your personal circumstances allow for flexibility.

- Provide an example where you have gone out of your way to help your employer. Tell them that you understand how important flexible working is to the role of a cabin crew member.

QUESTION NUMBER 6

What challenges will our airline face in the future and how could you, as a cabin crew member, help us to overcome these?

This type of question serves two main purposes for the panel. The first purpose is that it assesses how much you understand about the airline industry, in terms of its competitiveness.

The second purpose is that it assesses your awareness of how influential cabin crew staff are in their role.

Cabin crew are some of the most important employees of an airline. If passengers have a bad experience during a flight then they are unlikely to return to that airline. There are so many different airlines to choose from and competition is fierce, so staying ahead of the game and providing an exceptional level of service is important. Even if the airline is low budget, in terms of its airfare price, it is still important that the cabin crew staff are friendly, helpful and customer-focused.

Take a look at our sample response on the following page before constructing your own answer using a blank sheet of paper.

QUESTION NUMBER 6 – SAMPLE RESPONSE

What challenges will our airline face in the future and how could you, as a cabin crew member, help us to overcome these?

"The airline industry is extremely competitive and the expectations of the customer is always on the increase. People generally want to pay less for their service but still expect a high level of customer care.

In addition to the competitiveness of the modern day market, there is also the issue of security and the financial implications this has in terms of additional training and advanced security measures. The cost of fuel and salary expenses will continue to increase, which will undoubtedly have an effect on the cost of the product.

Therefore, it is important that cabin crew members provide the highest level of customer service at all times.

Customers are prepared to pay that little bit extra for a high quality service and the cabin crew staff are responsible for delivering it.

Ensuring the customer is satisfied with the service will mean they are far more likely to come back to the airline time and time again. More importantly however, they will recommend the airline to their friends and relatives."

KEY AREAS TO CONSIDER:

- Competitiveness of the industry, security issues and increased operating costs for the airline.

- High customer expectations and how cabin crew can help deliver this.

- A quality service means customers are far more likely to return and use the service again.

QUESTION NUMBER 7

Do you think you will find the change of lifestyle it difficult to adapt to, if you are successful in becoming a member of the cabin crew team?

There is only one answer to this question and that is 'No, it will not be difficult to adapt to'.

When answering questions of this nature, tell them that you have researched the role and are fully aware of the implications, including the change of lifestyle it will bring.

Also, remember to touch on the specifics about the change in lifestyle, what it means to you and how you have prepared for it.

Don't be afraid to say that some areas will be a challenge for you, but that you are fully committed and prepared for everything the job presents.

There now follows a sample response. Once again, read it and take any useful ideas from it. Then prepare your own based on your own individual circumstances.

QUESTION NUMBER 7 – SAMPLE RESPONSE

Do you think you will find the change of lifestyle it difficult to adapt to, if you are successful in becoming a member of the cabin crew team?

"Although this is something that I have dreamt of doing for many years now, I have still taken the time to look into the lifestyle change and how it will affect me.

Whilst some areas will be challenging, I am 100% confident I will not have any problems adapting. My personal circumstances are such that I can work the roster system comfortably and I am prepared for

being away from home for long periods, as and when required.

I have few personal commitments at home and am fully prepared for the lifestyle change, if I am successful in my application. In fact, I am very much looking forward to the change, as it is something I have wanted for a long time.

I live life to the full and my personality is one that is adaptable to most circumstances."

KEY AREAS TO CONSIDER:

- Smile and be enthusiastic in your response.

- Talk about the change in lifestyle for you and how you have prepared for it. You have thought long and hard about this career and your personal circumstances are suited to the role.

QUESTION NUMBER 8

How would you deal with somebody in a work situation who you felt was not pulling their weight and working as part of the team?

This type of question can be asked in a variety of formats.

You may be provided with a situation based around somebody not pulling their weight during a flight, or it may be a question asking you to provide an example of where you have dealt with this type of situation in your current or previous role.

Whichever is the case, the question is designed to assess your assertiveness and confidence, whilst being tactful. They are not looking for you to respond in a confrontational manner but, instead, looking for you to approach the person and resolve the issue with the minimum of fuss. To ignore the issue is not an option.

There now follows a response which gives an example of a work situation. Somebody is taking too many breaks and not pulling weight.

Once you have read the example, try to think of any experiences you have where you have had to deal with this type of issue. Then, use a blank sheet of paper to create a response.

QUESTION NUMBER 8 – SAMPLE RESPONSE

How would you deal with somebody in a work situation who you felt was not pulling their weight and working as part of the team?

"Whilst working in my current role as a waiter for a local restaurant, I was aware of a colleague who was taking more breaks than he was entitled to. Whilst he was

taking these additional breaks, the rest of the team would have to cover for the shortfall. Unfortunately, the customer would then suffer as the time it took for them to be served would increase. I decided to approach the person in order to resolve the issue. I walked over to him and asked him in a friendly manner if he would come and help the rest of team serve the customers. I told him that we were busy and that we needed his help. Fortunately, he responded in a positive manner and realised that he was taking advantage of his rest periods. Since then, there has not been an issue.

It is important that the team gets on and works well together. We cannot afford to have confrontational situations and the best way to resolve issues like this is to be honest and tactful."

KEY AREAS TO CONSIDER:

- Do not be confrontational.

- Be tactful in your approach, focusing on the customer as the priority. Effective teamwork is essential.

- Do not ignore the situation, but instead deal with it tactfully.

QUESTION NUMBER 9

How do you feel about working with people from different cultures and backgrounds?

This is quite a common interview question and one that you need to be prepared for. Respect for diversity is essential to the role of a cabin crew member. You will be working with both colleagues and customers from different cultures and backgrounds and, therefore, it is important that you are comfortable with this. We live in a diverse community that brings many positive aspects that we can learn from. When answering the question, you should be aiming to demonstrate that you are totally at ease when working with people from different cultures and backgrounds. You may wish to give an example of this in your response.

Take a look at the following response to this question before using a blank sheet of paper to construct your own answer to this type of question.

Remember to be honest in your reply and only state the facts about your feelings towards people from different cultures. If you are not truthful in your response, you will not be doing yourself, or the airline, any favours.

QUESTION NUMBER 9 – SAMPLE RESPONSE

How do you feel about working with people from different cultures and backgrounds?

> "*I am totally at ease in those situations, in fact I don't even think about it. This has never been a problem for me.*
>
> *I have a sincere interest in people from different*

cultures and backgrounds and have learnt many things from them in the past. I would like to think that we can all learn something from everybody, regardless of their culture or background and this is a part of the job that I would look forward to.

There are so many different and exciting things to learn in life and this can only be achieved by meeting, respecting and understanding people from different cultures and backgrounds. Teams that are diverse in nature have a better chance of delivering a higher quality of service. If the customer base is diverse, then so should the workforce that delivers the service."

KEY AREAS TO CONSIDER:

- Be honest when answering this type of question.

- Demonstrate that you understand diversity and the benefits this brings to society. Provide examples where appropriate.

QUESTION NUMBER 10

What is the best example of customer service that you have come across?

What is the best example of customer service that you have come across?

The majority of airlines pride themselves on their high level of service. However, some are better than others.

This type of question is designed to see how high your standards are, in relation to customer service. Those people who have a great deal of experience in a customer-focused environment will be able to answer this question with relative ease.

However, those who have little experience in this area will need to spend more time preparing their response.

Try to think of an occasion when you have witnessed an excellent piece of customer service and show that you learned from it. If you are very confident, then you may have an occasion when you, yourself, provided that service. Whatever response you provide, make sure it is unique and stands out.

There now follows a sample response that relates to an individual who went that extra mile to make certain the customer was happy.

Once you have read it, use a blank sheet of paper to create your own.

QUESTION NUMBER 10 – SAMPLE RESPONSE

What is the best example of customer service that you have come across?

"Whilst working as a shop assistant in my current role, a member of the public came in to complain to the manager about a pair of football shoes that he had bought for his son's birthday. When his son came to open the present on the morning of his birthday, he noticed that one of the football boots was a larger size than the other. He was supposed to be playing football with his friends that morning and wanted to wear his new boots. However, due to the shop's mistake, this was not possible. Naturally, the boy was very upset. The manager of the shop was excellent in her approach to dealing with situation. She remained calm throughout and listened to the gentleman very carefully, showing complete empathy for his son's situation. This immediately defused any potential confrontation. She then told him how sorry she was for the mistake that had happened, and that she would feel exactly the same if it was her own son who it had happened to. She then told the gentleman that she would refund the money in full and give his son a new pair of football boots to the same value as the previous pair. The man was delighted with her offer. Not only that, she then offered to give the man a further discount of 10% on any future purchase, due to the added inconvenience that was caused by him having to return to the shop to sort out the problem. I learned a lot from the way my manager dealt with this situation. She used exceptional communication skills and remained calm throughout. She then went

the extra mile to make the gentleman's journey back to the shop a worthwhile one.

The potential for losing a customer was averted by her actions and I feel sure the man would return to our shop again."

KEY AREAS TO CONSIDER:

- Use an example where somebody has gone the extra mile.

- Remember that part of the role of a cabin crew member is to provide a high level of customer service.

- Tell them what you learned from the experience.

QUESTION NUMBER 11

What do you think makes a successful cabin crew team?

Part of the role of a cabin crew member is to be a competent and effective team player. The purpose of this question is to assess your knowledge of what a team is and how it operates effectively. Some of the important aspects to remember, when operating as a cabin crew team member, are as follows:

- Gets on well with the rest of the team.

- Offers effective solutions to problem solving.

- Utilises effective listening skills both verbal and non-verbal.

- Makes an effort to involve others.

- Can be adaptable and willing to try others' ideas.

- Gives positive feedback to the rest of the team.

- When things are going wrong, remains positive and enthusiastic.

These are just a few examples of how a member of a team can help contribute in a positive way.

Now, take a look at the sample response that follows. Then use a blank sheet of paper to construct your own answer.

QUESTION NUMBER 11 – SAMPLE RESPONSE

What do you think makes a successful cabin crew team?

"There are a number of important elements that would make a successful cabin crew team. To begin with, it is

important to have different types of people in terms of their personalities, views and opinions. This way you are more likely to get a variety of options and solutions to problems when they arise.

The team members need to be positive, enthusiastic and have the ability to get on with each other. There should be no confrontation between members of the team and an understanding from everyone that they are working together to achieve a common goal of delivering a high quality service, and also ensuring the safety of all passengers.

Each member of the team should be a competent communicator and be able to listen to other people's ideas and opinions. Flexibility in the team is also important to try new and different ideas when appropriate.

Every team member should provide encouragement and work hard together when the pressure is on. Above all, cabin crew are role models for the airline, and each member of the team should uphold the values of their employer."

KEY AREAS TO CONSIDER:

- Utilise key words in your response.

- Demonstrate that you understand the qualities of an effective team.

- Remember the ultimate aim of delivering a high quality service and ensuring the safety of all passengers.

QUESTION NUMBER 12

Have you ever lost your temper?

This is a great interview question and is not easy to answer.

All of us have lost our temper at some point, but you need to be careful as to how much you disclose.

Part of the role of a cabin crew member is to remain calm under pressure and you need to demonstrate this in your response. They do not want to employ people who lose their temper at the slightest hint of confrontation. It is during these times that you will need to use your skills to defuse the conflict.

The question is designed to see how honest you are, and whether you are a naturally aggressive person. It is ok to lose your temper at times during your personal life, but it is not welcome as a cabin crew member.

How would it look if you saw a cabin crew member losing his/her temper during a flight? It would be embarrassing and unprofessional!

Take a look at the sample response that follows before taking the time to construct your own.

QUESTION NUMBER 12 – SAMPLE RESPONSE

Have you ever lost your temper?

> "In the whole I am a calm person and do not become aggressive or confrontational.
>
> Whilst it is only natural to be annoyed with people from time to time, I see no point in losing my temper.

It is just wasted energy.

I understand that cabin crew staff cannot lose their temper with passengers, it would be highly unprofessional. I appreciate that it must be frustrating at times dealing with difficult passengers, but the way to resolve issues is to remain calm and be patient."

KEY AREAS TO CONSIDER:

- Try to use 'non-confrontational' words and phrases during your response – patience, calm, understanding, etc.

- Demonstrate your understanding of the cabin crew's role and the importance of remaining calm and professional.

QUESTION NUMBER 13

If you were not successful today would you re-apply?

There is only one answer to this type of question and that is "Yes I would".

The question is designed to see how dedicated you are to their particular airline. The important thing to remember, when responding to this type of question, is to mention that you would look to improve on your weak areas for next time.

Determination is the key to success and if you are not accepted the first time, you will work hard to improve for the next time.

Most people, if asked this question think they have failed and are not going to be offered a job. Do not fall into this trap. It is a question that is designed to see how committed you are to joining their airline! Be positive in your response.

There now follows a sample response to this type of question.

Once you have read it, take the time to construct your own using a blank sheet of paper.

QUESTION NUMBER 13 – SAMPLE RESPONSE

If you were not successful today would you re-apply?

"Yes I would, most definitely. I have researched many different airlines and this is the one that I would like to join. If I am not successful at this attempt, then I will go away and look for ways to improve. Whilst I would be disappointed, I would not be negative about the situation. One of my qualities is that I have the ability to accept, and work on, my weaknesses. If there was

the option for feedback, I would take this up and improve on the areas I needed to work on.

However, I would love to be successful at this attempt and do believe that I am ready, now, to become a competent and professional cabin crew member with your airline."

KEY AREAS TO CONSIDER:

- The only real answer to this question is 'yes'.

- Be positive about the prospect of not being successful and tell them that you would work on your weaknesses.

- Don't be afraid to be confident in your own abilities.

QUESTION NUMBER 14

How many times have you called in sick within the last year?

This is an easy question to answer, but one that can do you some damage if you have a poor sickness record.

The ideal answer here is zero days. The airline need people who are reliable.

If a member of the cabin crew calls in sick on the day of their flight, this will cause problems for the airline. They then have to dedicate time and resources to phone around and find somebody else to cover for the sick person.

Genuine sickness cannot be avoided. However, in every job there are people who take advantage of sick leave, which costs employees thousands of pounds every year.

The airline industry is keen to avoid employing people who have a poor sickness record.

There now follows a sample response which is based on an individual who has no record of sickness within the last 12 months.

QUESTION NUMBER 14 – SAMPLE RESPONSE

How many times have you called in sick within the last year?

"I have had no days off sick within the last 12 months.

I am an honest person and would only ever call in sick if I really could not make it to work. I understand that the airline needs to employ reliable people and if a member of the team goes sick, you will need to find somebody else to cover for them."

KEY AREAS TO CONSIDER:

- The least day's sickness you have, the better.

- Be aware of the implications for the airline if an employee is constantly calling in sick.

- Genuine sickness cannot be avoided.

In the next section of the guide we will provide you with a useful section that will teach you how to deal with customer complaints, something which you will get asked about during the interview!

BE THE FIRST TO BE ALERTED WHEN CABIN CREW JOBS BECOME AVAILABLE!

Go to:

www.Cabin-Crew-Jobs.co.uk

to register your interest now…

Attend a Cabin Crew Training Course!

Go to:

www.cabincrewcourses.com

CHAPTER SEVEN
HOW TO DEAL WITH COMPLAINTS

DEALING WITH COMPLAINTS

Within the next few pages, we have provided you with some information on how to deal with complaints effectively. Try to imagine yourself as passenger on a flight.

The service has not been fantastic and you want to complain. Are you concerned the fact that one of the cabin crew staff went sick at the last minute and the crew are short? No, of course you're not. Neither are you concerned about the fact that other people are complaining at the other end of the aircraft. In fact, all you are concerned with is that your complaint gets dealt with quickly and effectively.

During your career as a cabin crew member, you will be faced with highly stressful situations in relation to difficult

customers and you will need to react appropriately.

In any industry or profession where a customer is complaining, there are 7 key areas that the complainant is concerned with:

- They want someone to listen to their complaint.

- They want someone to understand why they are complaining.

- They want someone to sort out their complaint as soon as possible.

- They would like an apology.

- They want someone to explain what has gone wrong.

Cabin crew members are required to deal with complaints in an efficient and effective manner. If you are successful in your application, your training course will cover these core skills in detail. However, having knowledge of how to deal with customer complaints during the selection process will assist you. You may be asked a question, during the interview, that relates to customer complaints and having the ability to explain how they are dealt with is a positive aspect. When dealing with customer complaints in any form, you will need to follow an action plan. This action plan is explained in detail on the following pages. The plan follows a structured format and each area follows on systematically from the other. To begin with, you will listen to the complaint using effective verbal and nonverbal listening skills. The majority of people associate communication skills primarily with the spoken word. However, these cover a number of areas. Having the ability to actively listen is a key factor to resolving the complaint successfully. Take a look at the stages of dealing with complaints before reading each individual section.

- Listen to the complaint.

- Apologise and appreciate.

- Gather information.

- Provide a solution.

- Reach an agreement.

- Take action.

- Follow up.

At the end of the explanations, we have provided you with a 'Dealing with Complaints' exercise to help you put these skills into practice.

LISTEN TO THE COMPLAINT

One of the most important factors, when dealing with the complaint, is to listen. Listening effectively can be done in a number of ways. This can be achieved through facial expression, body language, oral confirmation and clarification techniques.

If the passenger is sat down in their chair then you may wish to crouch down to their level. This will alleviate any confrontational body position where you are looking down at the complainant. This will also prevent the need for speaking any louder than necessary.

Then, listen to the complaint in full.

Maintain good eye contact throughout, nod, use an interested facial expression and confirm back to the passenger what they have told you. If the passenger begins to shout, becomes aggressive or confrontational, or even starts swearing, then

you will have to be assertive in your response and inform them that their language will not be tolerated. Inform them that you want to deal with their complaint quickly and to their satisfaction, but it must be done in a calm manner.

APOLOGISE AND APPRECIATE

Once you have listened to their complaint, you need to apologise and explain that you fully understand how they feel. This will usually have the effect of defusing any confrontation and will make the complainant feel that they are being heard. It is all about establishing a rapport with the passenger and making them feel that their complaint is important. The following is a sample response to a customer's complaint:

"Thank you for taking the time, sir, to explain what the problem is. If the same situation had happened to me I would certainly feel as you do."

In just two sentences, you have made the complainant feel valued and understood. Now you can begin to resolve the issue and you will find it easier to talk to them from now on.

Providing their complaint is genuine, you should now take ownership of the complaint and see it through to a successful resolution. You have listened to their complaint and acknowledged there is an issue. Now move on to establishing the facts, which will give you the tools to create a successful resolution.

GATHER INFORMATION

When dealing with a complaint as a cabin crew member, the next important stage is to gather as much essential

information as possible. The reason for doing this is that it will allow you to make a more informed judgement about the situation and it will also allow you to take steps to prevent it from happening again.

Complaints take time to deal with and detract you from other important duties. When a member of the team is dealing with a complaint, the rest of team must make up for the deficit in numbers. Therefore, if the situation that led to the complaint in the first instance can be avoided in the future, this will help the flight to run smoother and allow the cabin crew staff to concentrate on their primary role – providing a high level of customer service and ensuring the safety of all passengers.

When gathering information, concentrate on the following areas:

- What is the complaint in relation to?

- What are the facts of the incident?

- Who was responsible?

- How would the passenger like the problem to be resolved?

Once you have gathered all of the facts, you will then be able to take action to resolve the issue.

PROVIDE A SOLUTION

Coming up with a suitable solution to the customer's complaint can be difficult, especially if they are reluctant to accept any reasonable offering. Therefore, it is important that you remain calm throughout.

Make sure that the solution/s you offer are relevant to the

situation and are achievable. If they are not, then do not make the mistake of offering something you cannot deliver. This will just make the situation worse. When providing a solution, ask the customer if your offer is acceptable. For example:

"Would you like me to get you another drink?" or "Would you like me to see if we have an alternative meal?"

By offering different solutions to the complainant you are asking them to make the decision for you, and therefore making your life easier. This way, they will end up getting what they want and, therefore, will be happy with the resolution.

Remember – when dealing with the complaint, never take it personally and never be rude or confrontational.

REACH AN AGREEMENT

Once you have offered the solution, make sure you get the complainants approval first. This will prevent them from complaining about the action you are taking to resolve the issue. The most effective method of achieving this is through verbal acknowledgement.

For example:

"Ok sir, to resolve the issue, I will go away and get you another meal. I will make sure that the meal is hot. Is this alright with you?"

Reaching an agreement is important psychologically. The passenger will feel that you are being considerate to their needs and, by reaffirming the solution with them; you are showing them that you have their interests at heart.

TAKE ACTION

Plain and simple. Now that you have reached an agreement, get on with task in hand. If it is going to take you a while to take the action agreed upon, you might find it useful to inform the passenger.

"Ok, I will now go and get your meal. This might take me a few minutes, so please bear with me."

In the final section of the guide we will provide you with a useful contacts section to help you search for cabin crew jobs with the major airlines.

CHAPTER EIGHT
AIRLINE CONTACT DETAILS

Within this section of the guide we have provided airline contact details to make it easier for you to research and apply.

The majority of airlines provide recruitment information through their websites. When researching the role of both a cabin crew member and the airline, your first port of call should be the website. This will provide you with plenty of up-to-date information about the airline, its products and service, possible future developments and how they operate.

Take a piece of paper and a pen, and then spend some time studying the website of your chosen airline. Write down any information that will help you during your application.

You will also find that many airlines allow you to apply online through their online application form. If this is the case, remember to print off your completed form before

submitting it. You will need to make reference to it prior to the assessment centre.

Make sure to check that you meet the minimum requirements, of the airline you wish to apply for, before submitting your application form – many of them vary.

AIR ATLANTA
www.airatlanta.com

AIR WALES
www.airwales.com

BMI
www.flybmi.com

BRITANNIA AIRWAYS
www.britanniaairways.com

BRITISH AIRWAYS
www.britishairways.com

CITY EXPRESS
www.bacitiexpressjobs.com

EMIRATES
www.emiratesairline.com

EASY JET
www.easyjet.com

EXCEL AIRWAYS
www.xl.com

FIRST CHOICE
www.airline.recruitment@firstchoice.co.uk

FLYBE
www.flybe.com

FLYJET
www.flyjet.com

GB AIRWAYS
www.gbairways.co.uk

GULF AIR
www.gulfairco.com

IBERIA
www.iberia.com

JET2
www.jet2.com

MONARCH
www.flymonarch.com

MY TRAVEL
www.mytravel.com

QANTAS
www.quantas.com

THOMAS COOK
www.thomascook.com

UNITED
www.unitedairlines.co.uk

VIRGIN ATLANTIC
www.virgin-atlantic.com

how2become

Visit www.how2become.co.uk
to find more titles and courses that
will help you to pass the cabin crew
selection process:

- Online cabin crew tests

- Online cabin crew training courses

- Psychometric testing books and CDs.

www.how2become.co.uk

BE THE FIRST
TO BE ALERTED
WHEN CABIN CREW
JOBS BECOME
AVAILABLE!

Go to:

www.Cabin-Crew-Jobs.co.uk

to register your interest now…

Attend a Cabin Crew
Training Course!

Go to:

www.cabincrewcourses.com